TABLE OF CONTENTS

Introduction

Literally meaning "to touch your heart", dim sum is a Chinese eating custom which sprung from Cantonese teahouses. The art of Chinese dim sum rests on enjoying an assortment of Chinese goodies in small proportions while drinking your tea. In the olden days, travelers and farmers would often flock roadside teahouses after hours to relax while drinking their afternoon tea. Soon, these teahouses started serving small snacks with their tea, giving birth to the tradition of dim sum. Dim sum varies from savory to sweet to everything in between – anything goes! The three main types of dim sum include the dumplings, the bau (steamed or baked buns) and the spring rolls.

Delicious Dim sum: A Collection of Simple Chinese Dim Sum Recipes contains 35 authentic, delicious, and simple dim sum recipes that you'll surely love.

Dumplings

When you hear the word dim sum, the first thing that probably comes to mind is a little bamboo steamer basket filled with rows and rows of hot, steaming dumplings. These little pieces of dough are filled with meat, seafood or vegetables and are then steamed or sometimes fried. This section of the book will show you how to make delicious and tasty dumplings!

Har Gow

Plump and juicy shrimp encased in soft, dumpling skin...
yum! You can't ever go wrong with these traditional
dumpling fillings. If possible, try to get the freshest shrimps
you can buy to ensure the best-tasting dumplings you'll
ever have.

Makes 24 dumplings.

Ingredients:

- 24 pcs. dumpling wrappers (available in most Asian groceries.)
- 7 oz. package of dumpling wrappers (available in most Asian groceries.)

Filling

- 16 oz. shrimp, peeled and deveined
- 2 tbsp. bamboo shoots, minced
- 1 tbsp. green onions, minced
- 1 tsp. ginger, grated
- 2 tbsp. pork fat, minced
- 3 tsp. light soy sauce
- 2 tbsp. dry sherry
- 2 tsp. sugar
- 2 tsp. sesame oil
- 4 tsp. tapioca starch
- salt and pepper
- nappa cabbage leaves (for lining the steamer)
- light soy sauce for dipping

Directions:

1. In a big bowl, combine all the ingredients for the filling. Mix until everything is incorporated. Let them mixture stand in the refrigerator for 2 hours.

2. Start wrapping your dumplings. Begin by taking a spoonful of the filling and place it in the middle of the wrapper. Fold over and pleat the front side of the dumpling using your thumb and forefinger. Bring the back side forward and seal it with the front. Use water mixed with a little cornstarch to seal the dumpling. Repeat until you finished all the dumplings.

3. Line the steamer with nappa cabbage leaves. Place the dumplings on the lined steamer and cook for 10 minutes.

4. Remove from the steamer and arrange in a serving plate. Serve hot with light soy sauce for dipping.

Pork and Cabbage Dumplings

Who said you can't have your meat and your veggies, too? With these pork and cabbage-filled delights, you get to have the best of both! Give this super simple and delicious dumpling recipe a try.

Makes 24 dumplings.

Ingredients:

- 24 pcs. packaged dumpling wrappers (available in most Asian groceries.)

Filling

- 6 oz. nappa cabbage leaves, finely chopped
- 15 oz. ground pork
- ½ tsp. salt
- ½ tsp. ginger, finely grated
- 1/8 cup green onions, minced
- 1 tbsp. soy sauce
- ½ tbsp. Chinese rice wine
- 1 tsp. sesame oil
- dash of ground white pepper

Dipping sauce

- soy sauce
- rayu (Japanese chili oil)

Directions:

1. Place the cabbage in a large bowl and sprinkle with the salt. Let it sit for about 10 minutes.

2. Meanwhile, combine in your food processor the ginger, green onions, ground pork, soy sauce, rice wine, sesame oil and pepper. Pulse the processor a few times to mix the ingredients well. Set aside.

3. Return to the cabbage and using your hands, squeeze out the excess water. Fold in the squeezed cabbage to the pork mixture.

4. Start wrapping your dumplings. Begin by taking a spoonful of the filling and place it in the middle of the

wrapper. Fold over and pleat the front side of the dumpling using your thumb and forefinger. Bring the back side forward and seal it with the front. Use water mixed with a little cornstarch to seal the dumpling. Repeat until you finished all the dumplings.

5. To cook, half fill a large pot with water and bring it to a boil. When it starts boiling, gently slide in half of the dumplings. Let it simmer and gently cook for 6-8 minutes. Remove the dumplings from the water with a slotted spoon. Repeat with the remaining dumplings. Serve hot with soy sauce and rayu.

Gyoza

Widely popular in Japan, gyoza is actually of Chinese origin and is a delightful meat-filled treat. They are flatter than the typical dumpling and may either be served steamed or pan-fried. For this recipe, the gyoza is pan-fried to give them that slight crunch. But if you prefer, you can serve them right after steaming.

Makes 24 dumplings.

Ingredients:

- 24 pcs. packaged gyoza wrappers (available in most Asian groceries)

Filling

- ½ nappa cabbage, leaves separated
- 3 oz. chives, finely chopped
- 3 cloves garlic, crushed
- 6 pcs. shiitake mushrooms, soaked and chopped finely
- 15 oz. ground pork
- ½ tbsp. sesame oil
- ½ tbsp. black bean garlic sauce (available in most Asian groceries)
- ½ tbsp. sugar
- 2 tbsp. soy sauce
- 3 tbsp. oil for frying

Vinegar dip

- ¼ cup vinegar
- ¼ cup soy sauce
- chili oil

Directions:

1. Boil the cabbage until tender. Drain and chop finely.

2. In a large bowl, combine together all the ingredients for the filling. Mix well.

3. Start wrapping your dumplings. Begin by taking a spoonful of the filling and place it in the middle of the wrapper. Fold over and pleat the front side of the dumpling using your thumb and forefinger. Bring the back side forward and seal it with the front. Use water mixed with a

little cornstarch to seal the dumpling. Repeat until you finished all the dumplings.

4. * Heat the oil for frying in a shallow, non-stick frying pan at medium heat. Pan fry the gyoza until the bottom is slightly browned. While waiting for the gyoza to be cooked, boil about a cup of water.

5. When the bottom part has browned, add the boiling water to cover the whole pan. Place a lid and let it steam until the meat is completely cooked. Remove the lid and let the remaining water evaporate. Drain if there is too much liquid. Remove from the heat. Serve hot with the vinegar dip and chili oil. To make the vinegar dip, combine the vinegar and the soy sauce.

*Alternatively, you may simply steam the gyoza in a steamer for around 20 minutes or until the meat is cooked through. Line the steamer with cabbage leaves to ensure that they won't stick to the bottom.

Shui Jiao

Literally meaning 'water dumplings,' these delectable delights encase a yummy shrimp and chive filling. Cooked like the gyoza, shui jiao is tasty and slightly crispy treat that you'll surely enjoy!

Makes 4 servings.

Ingredients:

- 30 pcs. gyoza wrappers
- 2 tbsp. peanut oil
- ¼ cup water

Filling

- 8 oz. shrimp, peeled, deveined and chopped
- 3 tbsp. chives, chopped
- 1/8 cup water chestnuts, diced
- 1 tbsp. oyster sauce
- 1 tbsp. Shaoxing rice wine
- dash of salt and ground white pepper

Dipping sauce

- 2 tbsp. light soy sauce
- 2 tbsp. rice vinegar
- 2 tsp. sesame oil
- ¼ cup cilantro leaves, chopped

Directions:

1. In a bowl, mix the shrimp, chives, water chestnuts, oyster sauce and rice wine. Sprinkle with salt and pepper. Mix well. Set aside.

2. Make the dipping sauce. In another bowl, combine the soy sauce, rice vinegar, sesame oil and cilantro. Mix well. Set aside.

3. Begin wrapping your dumplings. Take spoonful of the filling and place it in the middle of the wrapper. Fold over and pleat the front side of the dumpling using your thumb and forefinger. Bring the back side forward and seal it with the front. Use water mixed with a little cornstarch to seal the dumpling. Repeat until you finished all the dumplings.

4. To cook, heat the peanut oil in a wok over medium heat. Place the dumplings standing up in the oil. Cook, uncovered, until the bottoms are a pale golden brown. Add the water around the edges of the wok, then cover. Cook until the liquid has evaporated, approximately 5 minutes. Serve warm together with the dipping sauce.

Gow Gee

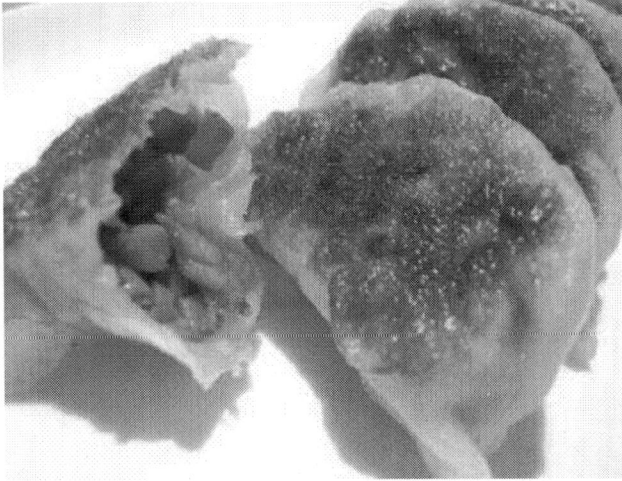

This recipe is quite similar to gyoza. The main difference lies in the manner of cooking. Gow gees are traditionally deep fried, giving it that crispier skin. Yum!

Makes 20 pieces.

Ingredients:

- 20 pcs. wonton wrappers
- 3 pcs. shiitake mushrooms, soaked and chopped
- 3 oz. shrimp, shelled and deveined
- 3 oz. pork
- 2 tbsp. bamboo shoots, drained and chopped
- 1 cup water
- ½ tsp. salt
- 2 water chestnuts, chopped
- 2 green onions, chopped
- 2 tsp. ginger, minced
- 1 tsp. sesame oil

- 1 ½ tsp. rice vinegar
- 1 tsp. soy sauce
- 1 tsp. sugar
- oil for deep-frying
- chili sauce

Directions:

1. Place the water in a bowl. Add the salt and dissolve. Soak the shrimp in this solution for 5 minutes. Drain and pat dry using paper towels. Set aside.

2. In a medium bowl, combine pork, bamboo shoots, water chestnuts, green onions, ginger, sesame oil, rice vinegar, soy sauce and sugar. Mix well.

3. Begin wrapping your gow gees. To wrap, first lay a piece of the wrapper on a clean surface. Place a teaspoon of filling in the middle. With moistened fingers, wet all the edges. Carefully fold the wonton over the filling and seal. Lightly pinch the edges to seal. Repeat for the remaining filling.

4. Heat enough oil in a wok. Make sure that it can completely cover the gow gees. Deep fry the gow gees, a few at a time, until they turn golden brown. Remove from heat. Drain excess oil on paper towels. Serve warm with chili sauce.

Chive Dumplings

Chives take the center stage with this dumpling! Combined with handmade dumpling wrapper, you'll surely enjoy its sharp and tart taste. Give it a try!

Makes 32 dumplings.

Ingredients:

- Wheat dough dumpling wrapper
- 1 cup wheat starch (plus some extra for dusting the kneading board)
- ¼ cup tapioca flour
- 1 cup chicken broth, heated
- ¼ tsp. salt
- 1 tsp. vegetable oil

21

Directions:

1. Place all the dry ingredients in a bowl. Stir in the hot chicken broth and vegetable oil. Give it a quick mix to incorporate all the ingredients using a wooden spoon.

2. Sprinkle wheat starch over a flat, kneading surface. While the dough is still hot, start kneading the dough until it becomes smooth. Add more wheat starch if the dough is too sticky.

3. Cut the dough into 4 equal sections. Using your palms, roll each section into a cylinder. Cut each cylinder into 8 pieces. Cover dough with plastic to avoid drying out the dough.

4. To make the wrapper, place a piece of dough between two pieces of parchment paper. Using the bottom of a pan, flatten the dough. Roll them out using a rolling pin until each piece is about 3-4 inches wide. Cover the wrappers with plastic while you make the filling.

Filling

- 1 ½ tsp. salt
- 7 oz. chives, chopped
- 7 oz. shrimps, peeled, deveined, and diced
- 1/3 cup bamboo shoots
- ½ tsp. soy sauce
- 1 tsp. sugar
- ½ tsp. toasted sesame oil
- 1 tsp. cornstarch
- 1 tbsp. cooking oil for frying

Directions:

1. Boil some water in a medium-sized pot. Take off from heat and blanch the chives, adding a teaspoon of the salt. Drain and rinse the chives under cold, running water. Squeeze the excess water out.

2. In a medium bowl, combine the chives, shrimp, bamboo shoots, soy sauce, the remaining salt, sugar, sesame oil and cornstarch. Mix just until all the ingredients are incorporated. Do not over mix.

3. Start wrapping your dumplings. Begin by taking a spoonful of the filling and place it in the middle of the wrapper. Fold over and pleat the front side of the dumpling using your thumb and forefinger. Bring the back side forward and seal it with the front. Use water mixed with a little cornstarch to seal the dumpling. Repeat until you finished all the dumplings.

4. Heat the cooking oil in a large skillet over medium-high heat. As soon as the skillet starts smoking, add the dumplings. Do not crowd your skillet otherwise they will stick together. Cook each side for about 2 minutes or until they are lightly browned. Add about 1/3 cup of water and cover with a lid. Let it steam until the filling is completely cooked and the water has evaporated.

5. Remove the lid and raise the heat back to medium. When the water has evaporated, flip the dumplings over and brown the other side. Serve them hot.

Taro Dumplings

Taro for your dumpling wrapper? Well this is certainly a novel idea and the taro gives your wrapper that distinctive taste. Give it a try!

Makes 24 dumplings.

Ingredients:

- Taro dumpling wrapper
- 14 oz. taro root, peeled and diced
- 7 oz. wheat starch
- 2 ½ tbsp. cornstarch
- 4 tsp. baking powder
- 2 tbsp. sugar
- 1 tsp. ground white pepper
- dash of salt
- 10 oz. boiling water
- 10 tbsp. shortening

Directions:

1. Set up your steamer and steam the taro root for 20 or until they turn soft. Transfer contents in a deep, flat-bottomed dish, and mash it while it is still hot. Let it cool for a couple of minutes. Set aside.

2. Meanwhile, sift together the wheat starch, cornstarch and baking powder in a bowl. Then, add the boiling water to the flour mixture. Mix well while it is still hot.

3. Add the mashed taro into the dough. Knead until taro and flour are well mixed.

4. Add the sugar, pepper and salt. Mix well. Then, add the shortening and blend it to make smooth dough. Wrap the dough with plastic. Refrigerate for at least 2 hours.

Filling

- 4 pcs. shiitake mushrooms, soaked and diced
- 4oz. pork shoulders, diced
- 2 oz. shrimp, peeled, deveined, and diced
- 2 scallion, sliced thinly
- 4 tsp. peanut oil
- 1 tsp. soy sauce
- 1 tsp. rice wine
- 1 tsp. sesame oil
- ½ tsp. salt
- ¼ tsp. ground white pepper
- 2 tsp. cornstarch dissolved in 2 tbsp. cold water
- vegetable oil for deep frying

Directions:

1. Heat the peanut oil in a large skillet over high heat. When it is almost smoking, add the pork, shrimp, mushrooms, and scallion, and stir-fry for 2 minutes. Add the soy sauce, rice wine, sesame oil, salt, and white pepper and continue stir-frying for a minute.

2. Stir in the cornstarch mixture and cook for 30 seconds longer, or until it thickens. Remove the mixture from the heat and let it cool. Set aside.

3. Take your dough from the fridge and divide it into 24 equal pieces. Wet your hands and hold one lump of dough in your palm. Flatten it slightly then put about 2-3 tablespoons of the filling onto the center. Mold the dough completely around the filling into a football shape. Repeat for the remaining dough and filling.

4. Heat oil in a deep fryer. Fry dumplings until they turn golden brown. Do not crowd your fryer. Drain excess oil with paper towels. Serve hot.

Shuumai

Probably one of the more popular dumpling recipes, shuumai is simply a steamed pork-filled dumpling, served with a chili soy sauce dipping sauce.

Makes 24 dumplings.

Ingredients:

- 24 pcs. shuumai or wonton wrappers (available in most Asian groceries.)
- Filling
- 9 oz. ground pork
- ¼ cup jicama, minced
- ¼ cup carrots, minced
- 1 small onion, minced
- 2 leeks, chopped
- 1 egg
- 1 tbsp. sesame oil
- ½ tsp. ground pepper

- ½ tsp. salt
- 1 tsp. sugar

Dipping sauce

- soy sauce
- chili oil

Directions:

1. Place all the ingredients for the filling in a large bowl. Mix well. Set aside.

2. Separate the wrappers. To wrap your shuumai, spoon a tablespoon of mixture into the middle each wrapper. Fold the edges toward each other and seal with water.

3. Brush your steamer basket with oil. Arrange the shuumai in the steamer basket. Make sure there is enough space between each shuumai so they won't stick to each other. Do not place it on your steamer yet.

4. Boil water for steaming. When it starts boiling, place the steamer basket and steam the shuumai for 15-20 minutes. Remove from heat. Serve hot together with the dipping sauce.

Eggplant Shuumai

Easy and yummy, what more can you ask for, right? These eggplant-filled delights are perfect with tea.

Makes 24 dumplings.

Ingredients:

- 24 pcs. shuumai or wonton wrappers (available in most Asian groceries.)

Filling

- 4 cups eggplant, peeled and chopped
- 2 tsp. canola oil
- 4 cloves garlic, minced
- 2 tsp. ginger, minces
- 2 tbsp. light soy sauce
- 1 tbsp. black bean sauce (available in most Asian groceries.)
- 1 tsp. sesame oil
- 4 tbsp. fresh cilantro, minced
- cornstarch for dusting

Chili Sauce

- 2 tbsp. soy sauce
- 1 tbsp. lime juice
- 1 tsp. honey
- 1 clove garlic, minced
- 1 tsp. ginger, grated
- 1 red jalapeño pepper, sliced thinly

Directions:

1. Heat oil over medium-high heat in a non-stick pan. Stir fry the garlic and ginger. Add the eggplant and continue stir fry over high heat until the eggplants turn soft.

2. Add the soy sauce, bean sauce, sesame oil and cilantro. Continue cooking until the mixture becomes thick. Remove from heat and let cool. Set aside.

3. Dust your working surface with cornstarch. Separate the wrappers. To wrap your shuumai, spoon a tablespoon of mixture into the middle each wrapper. Fold the edges toward each other and seal with water. Cover with plastic and chill in the fridge for about an hour.

4. Meanwhile, make your chili sauce. Mix all the ingredients in a bowl. Stir well. Transfer contents into serving bowls.

5. To cook your dumplings, prepare first your steamer. Brush the steamer basket with oil and place shuumai. Make sure there is enough space in between to prevent sticking. Steam the shuumai for about 8-10 minutes. Remove from heat. Serve warm together with the chili sauce.

Mushroom Shuumai

Here's a unique variation on the shuumai . Instead of using shuumai wrappers, mushrooms are used as wrapper and filling, too! Not only is it delicious, it also makes for a pretty presentation.

Makes about 12.

Ingredients:

- 12 pcs. whole chanterelle mushrooms (or any big, thin type of mushroom)
- 7 oz. button mushrooms, blanched
- 3 oz. shrimp, shelled and deveined
- 3 oz. ground pork
- 1 tsp. parsley, chopped
- 1 tsp. ham, minced
- 1 tsp. corn flour

Marinade

- ½ tsp. Chinese cooking wine
- ¼ tsp. salt
- ¼ tsp. pepper
- ½ tsp. sesame oil
- 1 tsp. light soy sauce
- ¾ tsp. sugar

Directions:

1. Place the shrimp in a flat, deep container. With your masher or a fork, mash the shrimp. Set aside.

2. Take a small bowl and combine all the marinade ingredients. Soak the shrimp, mushroom and ground pork in the marinade for at least half an hour.

3. Turn the mushrooms upside down with the gills facing upwards. Dust each piece with a little corn flour. Place the mushrooms into muffin cups for easier handling.

4. Stuff the filling into each mushroom. Garnish with the minced ham and chopped parsley.

5. Steam the shuumai for 10-15 minutes. Remove from heat and serve.

Pork Wonton

While wonton is often found as a noodle topping, it also tastes great on its own. Filled with chestnuts and pork, these wontons are definitely one of the best tasting ones you'll ever find!

Makes 4 servings.

Ingredients:

- 1 package wonton wrappers (available in most Asian groceries)
- 4 oz. ground pork
- ½ tsp. salt
- ½ tbsp. light soy sauce
- 2 oz. water chestnuts, drained and chopped
- 1 oz. bamboo shoots, drained and chopped
- 2 spring onions, chopped
- 2 oz. bean sprouts, chopped
- 1 egg, beaten

- 1 tbsp. Chinese rice wine
- oil for deep frying

Directions:

1. In a big bowl, combine the pork, salt, soy sauce, water chestnuts, bamboo shoots, spring onions, bean sprouts, egg, and rice wine. Mix well.

2. Place a teaspoon of the filling mixture in the centre of each wonton wrapper. Fold the edges toward each other and seal with water.

3. Heat the oil in a fryer over high heat. Deep fry the wontons until they are a light golden brown. Do not overcrowd your fryer. Remove from heat and drain excess oil with paper towels. Serve warm.

Apricot and Ginger Wonton

Wonton for dessert? Why not! This sweet, fruity and crispy concoction is not only perfect as a dessert it's also quite good with tea. Perfect for dim sum time!

Makes 16 wontons.

Ingredients:

- 16 pcs. wonton wrappers

Filling

- ½ cup dried apricots, chopped
- ¼ cup roasted cashews, chopped
- ¼ cup crystallized ginger, chopped
- 2 tbsp. raisins, chopped
- ½ tbsp. brown sugar
- 1 egg, lightly beaten

- vegetable oil for deep frying
- cornstarch for dusting pan
- cinnamon sugar

Orange Honey Sauce

- ½ cup fresh orange juice
- ½ cup honey
- 2 tbsp. orange zest

Directions:

1. In a bowl, combine the apricots, cashews, ginger, raisins and brown sugar. Mix well.

2. Dust your working surface with cornstarch. Place a won ton wrapper on your working surface. Place a spoonful of filling in the middle of the wrapper. Fold the edges toward each other and seal edges with the egg. Cover with plastic and chill in the fridge for half an hour.

3. Meanwhile, make your sauce. In a small saucepan, combine all the ingredients. Bring it to a simmer while stirring constantly. Continue for about 5 minutes. Remove from heat and let cool. Set aside.

4. Take your fryer and heat the oil. Fry the won tons until they are golden brown. Drain excess oil Dust won tons with sugar. Serve warm with the prepared sauce.

Crunchy Shrimp Balls

Shrimp is already delicious all on its own but what happens when you fry them into crispy little balls? Magic!

Makes 12 balls.

Ingredients:

- 6 pcs. spring roll skins
- 8 oz. shrimp, peeled, deveined and chopped
- ½ tsp. salt
- 1 tbsp. egg white, lightly beaten
- 1/8 tsp. white pepper

- ½ tsp. sugar
- ¼ tsp. sesame oil
- 1 ½ tsp. canola oil
- 1 ½ tsp. cornstarch
- 1 tsp. chives, finely chopped
- oil for deep frying
- chili garlic sauce (available in most Asian groceries)

Directions:

1. Place chopped shrimp over paper towels and pat to remove excess moisture. Set aside.

2. In a bowl, stir together salt, egg white, pepper, sugar, sesame oil, canola oil, and cornstarch. Add the shrimp. Stir well.

3. Transfer mixture into a food processor. Grind to a coarse texture. Add the chives. Grind again until it becomes a sticky, smooth paste. Transfer to a bowl and refrigerate for at least half an hour.

4. Meanwhile, separate each spring roll skin. Then, cut them into ¼ inch strips. Set aside.

5. Take your shrimp mixture and shape them into 1 inch-sized balls. Use two spoons to shape your balls. The mixture will let you make 12 balls.

6. Place the spring roll strips in a plate. Take a shrimp ball and roll it around the pile to make the strips stick. You may snip extra bits of the skins if you want. Repeat until all the balls are coated.

7. Heat the oil in your fryer over medium-high heat. Make sure that the oil will be enough to cover the shrimp balls. Fry the balls until they turn golden brown. Do not overcrowd your fryer. Remove from the oil and drain off excess oil with paper towels. Let cool and serve with the chili garlic sauce.

Crab Rangoon

A Chinese-American concoction, these delightful deep-fried dumplings are a heavenly mixed of cream cheese and flaky, crab meat. Simply delicious!

Makes 20 dumplings

Ingredients:

- 20 wonton wrappers
- 8 oz. cream cheese, at room temperature
- 3 oz. crab meat, flaked
- 1 tbsp. sugar
- 1 tsp. salt
- oil for deep frying
- sweet and sour sauce

Directions:

1. In a bowl, mix together the cream cheese, crab meat, sugar, and salt. Mix well.

2. Place a tablespoon of the filling in the middle of a wonton wrapper. Fold the ends of the wonton wrapper together, to make a tiny parcel. Pinch to seal tight. Use a little water to make sure that the filling won't seep out.

3. Heat the oil in a pan. Make sure that it will be deep enough to completely cover the crab rangoon. Deep fry until golden brown. Remove from heat. Drain off excess oil using paper towels. Serve hot together with the sweet and sour sauce.

Rolls

Dim sum is not just limited to dumplings! Rolls are also a popular type of dim sum. Roll fillings such as meat, vegetables or a combination of such are wrapped in thinner flour or rice-based wrappers and are often deep fried. Give these super simple and delicious recipes a try!

Egg Roll

Undoubtedly, egg rolls are tops on the dim sum rolls list! These savory, crunchy delights are perfect not only for dim sum but as appetizers as well.

Makes 24 rolls.

Ingredients:

- 24 pcs. egg roll wrappers

Filling

- 12 oz. pork, trimmed and cut into strips
- 2 tbsp. soy sauce
- 1 tbsp. Chinese cooking sherry
- 2 tsp. cornstarch
- 4 tbsp. vegetable oil
- 1 cup green onions, cut into strips
- 4 cups cabbage
- 2 cups mug bean sprouts
- 1 cup bamboo shoots, cut into strips
- 1 cup mushrooms, stems removed and cut into strips
- 1 egg white, beaten
- 3 cups vegetable oil for frying

Dipping sauce

- sweet and sour sauce or hoisin sauce

Directions:

1. Take a medium-sized bowl and mix together the pork, soy sauce, sherry, and cornstarch. Set aside.

2. In a pan, heat the 4 tablespoons of vegetable oil on high heat. Add half of the green onions and stir fry for a couple of minutes. Add the cabbage and bean sprouts and continue stir frying until they are wilted. Transfer into a small bowl and set aside.

3. Using the same pan, stir fry the pork till it's almost cooked through. Add the cabbage, sprouts, mushrooms and bamboo shoots. Sauté until cooked. Remove from heat. Drain any excess liquid from the pan.

4. To wrap you rolls, place a wrapper on a clean, working surface. Place about 2 tablespoons of filling near the corner of the wrapper closest to you. Adjust the amount of filling if your wrapper is a bit larger. Fold that corner over the filling. Then, fold the sides over toward the center. Roll the rest up toward the far corner. Wash the edges of the far corner with the beaten egg white to gently seal the egg roll. Repeat for the remaining filling.

5. To cook, heat the oil in a medium-sized pan. Fry a couple of egg rolls at a time until it turns golden brown. Use paper towels to drain off excess oil. Serve hot with your preferred dipping sauce.

Sweet Bean Paste Rolls

Sweet bean paste can also make for a delicious roll filling! This sweet dish is a perfect accompaniment for tea or as a unique dessert.

Makes 12 rolls.

Ingredients:

- 12 pcs. spring roll wrappers
- 17 oz. sweet red bean paste (available in most Asian groceries)
- oil for deep frying
- powdered sugar for dusting

Directions:

1. Place a wrapper on a clean, working surface. Place about 2 tablespoons of filling near the corner of the wrapper closest to you. Adjust the amount of filling if your wrapper is a bit larger. Fold that corner over the filling. Then, fold the sides over toward the center. Roll the rest up toward the far corner. Wash the edges of the far corner with the beaten egg white to gently seal the egg roll. Repeat for the remaining filling.

2. Heat the oil in a medium-sized pan. Fry a couple of pieces a time until they turn golden brown. Drain off excess oil with paper towels. Dust with powdered sugar before serving.

Firecracker Shrimp

Love spicy food? Then this recipe is for you! Spicy shrimp wrapped in spring roll skins and fried to a crisp, golden brown perfection. Can you say yummy?

Ingredients:

- 20 pcs. medium-sized shrimps, shelled and deveined but leave the tail on
- 20 pcs. spring roll skins
- 1 scallion, chopped finely
- ½ red chili, chopped finely
- 1 egg white, lightly beaten
- oil for deep frying

Marinade

- 1 tsp. ginger juice
- 1/8 tsp. salt
- ¼ tsp. sugar
- ¼ tsp. lime juice
- ¼ tbsp. sesame oil
- ¼ tsp. sesame seeds
- ¼ tsp. corn starch
- 1 tsp. ground white pepper

Directions:

1. With a paper towel, pat dry the shrimps. Set aside.

2. In a medium-sized mixing bowl, combine all the marinade ingredients. Soak the shrimps in the marinade for at least 20 minutes. Then, add in the scallion and red chili. Marinate for a further 5 minutes.

3. Place a wrapper on a clean, flat surface. Place a shrimp on one end and fold over to completely encase it. Fold the sides toward the middle. Seal with beaten egg white. Repeat for the remaining shrimps.

4. Heat the oil in a frying pan. Deep fry the shrimp until it turns a light, golden brown. Serve hot.

Fresh Spring Rolls

A medley of vegetables is encased in thin, rice wrappers makes for a nice deviation from its deep-fried version. Popular in the northern part of China, spring rolls can make for a good, light snack too!

Makes 20 rolls.

Ingredients:

- 20 sheets fresh spring roll wrapper (available in most Asian groceries)
- 1 lettuce, washed and dried
- 2 beaten eggs, fried and sliced into thin strips
- 1/8 cup cooking oil

Filling

- 2 cloves garlic, chopped
- 8 oz. French bean, sliced diagonally
- 8 oz. carrots, julienned
- 20 oz. jicama, julienned
- 1 tsp. salt
- ½ tsp. sugar
- ¼ tsp. ground white pepper

Sauce

- 5 pcs. red chilies, seeded
- 4 tbsp. sugar
- 4 tbsp. hot water
- 1 tbsp. vinegar
- ½ tsp. salt
- 1 tbsp. hoisin sauce

Directions:

1. Wash the jicama and carrot under cold, running water to remove excess starch. Drain well with a kitchen towel. Set aside.

2. Heat the oil in a wok. Add the garlic and quickly stir fry. Add the French beans, carrots and jicama . Continue stir frying.

3. Season with salt, sugar and pepper. Mix well. Reduce heat let it simmer for 2 minutes. Remove from heat. Set aside.

4. Prepare the sauce. Place the chilies in a blender. Blend until smooth.

5. Dissolve the sugar in water. Add the vinegar, salt and hoisin sauce and the sugar mixture into the blender. Process until everything is mixed in well. Set aside.

6. To prepare the spring rolls, place a piece of wrapper on a clean surface. Then, place a piece of lettuce on the lower part of the wrapper. Spread about a tablespoon of the sauce on top of the lettuce. Take your vegetable filling and place about a tablespoon between the sauce and the lettuce. Place a few strips of fried egg on top.

7. Working quickly, fold the lower part of the wrapper to fully covering the fillings. Then, fold in both sides toward the center. Roll to the end of the wrapper and place them on a serving plate. Serve immediately.

Bean Sprouts Fresh Spring Roll

Taking a cue from the first fresh spring roll recipe, this variation calls for bean sprouts and bean curd.

The contrast between the crunchy sprouts and softer bean curd makes a delicious taste!

Makes 20 rolls.

Ingredients:

- 20 sheets fresh spring roll wrapper (available in most Asian groceries)
- 1 lettuce, washed and dried
- 2 beaten eggs, fried and sliced into thin strips
- 1/8 cup cooking oil
- 2 cloves garlic, chopped
- ½ cup oyster sauce

Filling

- 8 oz. bean sprouts, cleaned and tails removed
- 9 oz. bean curd, washed, drained and cubed
- 1 tsp. salt
- ½ tsp. sugar

Directions:

1. Heat the oil in wok. Toss in the bean curd cubes and cook over high heat for 3 minutes.

2. Add the garlic, bean sprouts, salt and sugar. Mix well. Reduce heat and cook for another 2 minutes. Remove from heat.

3. To prepare the spring rolls, place a piece of wrapper on a clean surface. Then, place a piece of lettuce on the lower part of the wrapper. Spread about a tablespoon of oyster sauce on top of the lettuce. Take your vegetable filling and place about a tablespoon between the sauce and the lettuce.

7. Working quickly, fold the lower part of the wrapper to fully covering the fillings. Then, fold in both sides toward the center. Roll to the end of the wrapper and place them on a serving plate. Serve immediately.

Crab Rolls

Another fresh spring roll variation! This time a combination of crab meat, rice and avocadoes are wrapped in thin, spring roll wrappers. Give it a try!

Makes 8 rolls.

Ingredients:

- 8 pcs. spring roll wrappers
- 9 oz. fresh crab meat, cooked and flaked
- ¼ cup rice, freshly cooked
- ½ avocado, cut into 8 pieces
- 2 tbsp. rice vinegar
- 1 tsp. sugar
- 8 leaves of iceberg lettuce
- ½ cucumber, peeled, seeded and cut into strips
- ½ cup roasted red capsicums, sliced
- 4 tsp. lime juice

Directions:

1. Sprinkle the vinegar and sugar over the rice. Stir to combine. Set aside.

2. To make the rolls, place a leaf on a wrapper. Place a scoop of rice in the center of the lettuce. Then, add a spoonful of crab, a cucumber strip, an avocado slice and a capsicum strip. Sprinkle with lime juice. Fold the sides of the wrapper over the filling, then roll the wrapper up tightly around the filling. Repeat for the remaining rolls. Serve immediately.

Baked Pork Spring Rolls

Like the cooked spring rolls but hate the oily aftertaste? Well, these baked spring rolls are just right for you! It has the same crispy texture as its fried version minus the oil.

Makes 12 rolls.

Ingredients:

- 12 pcs. spring roll wrappers
- 8 oz. ground pork
- 2 oz. cabbage, shredded
- 1 oz. carrot, chopped
- 2 spring onions, chopped
- 2 tbsp. fresh coriander, minced
- ½ tsp. sesame oil
- ½ tbsp. oyster sauce
- 1 tsp. ginger, grated
- 1 ½ tsp. garlic. minced
- 1 red chili, seeded and chopped
- 1 tbsp. corn starch dissolved in 1 tbsp. water
- 2 tbsp. vegetable oil

Directions:

1. Pre-heat oven to 428° F.

2. Heat a non-stick fry pan. Cook the pork until it is lightly browned. Remove from heat. Drain off any excess fat and oil.

3. In a bowl, combine the pork, cabbage, carrot, spring onion, coriander, sesame oil, oyster sauce, ginger, garlic and chilies. Mix well.

4. To wrap you rolls, place a wrapper on a clean, working surface. Place about 1 tablespoon of filling near the corner of the wrapper closest to you. Adjust the amount of filling if your wrapper is a bit larger. Fold that corner over the filling. Then, fold the sides over toward the center. Roll the rest up toward the far corner. Moisten the edges of the far corner with the corn starch to seal. Repeat for the remaining filling.

5. Place the spring rolls on a medium baking sheet. Brush with vegetable oil. Bake in the pre-heated oven for 25 minutes or until lightly browned. Serve warm.

Bau

Soft, white fluffy dough encasing savory or sweet filling…
that's what a bau is! Often made from wheat flour, these
delicious, fluffy buns are a traditional main stay in any dim
sum set-up. They are also a favorite breakfast or mid-
morning snack. Mostly baked or steamed, give these
delicious bau recipes a try!

Char Shiu Bau

Char shiu or sweet, roasted pork wrapped in pillow-like soft buns. Now, that's a feast in itself!

Makes 12 buns.

Ingredients:

- Bau
- 1 cup warm water
- ½ cup water
- ¼ oz. active dry yeast
- 1 cup wheat flour
- 3 cups flour
- ¼ cup sugar
- 2 tbsp. shortening
- 1 ½ tsp. salt

Filling

- 3 cups char shiu, sliced thinly

Directions:

1. In a large bowl, stir together the warm water and yeast. Let rest for about 10 minutes to allow the yeast to proof.

2. Mix in the wheat flour into the yeast mixture until smooth. Cover with plastic wrap and set in a warm place to rise for about 1 hour.

3. Meanwhile, combine the sugar, shortening and ½ cup of water in a small saucepan. Bring to a boil over medium heat. Stir the mixture to dissolve the sugar. Remove from heat and set aside.

4. When the mixture has cooled, pour it into the batter mixture. Stir in the 3 cups of flour.

5. Lightly flour your kneading surface. Knead to form a soft, smooth dough. Place the dough into a large, greased bowl. Cover with a damp cloth and let it rise for about an hour or until the dough has doubled in size.

6. Punch down the dough with your fist and knead gently for another couple of minutes. Divide the dough into two equal halves. Roll each half into a log.

7. Cut each log into 12 pieces. Roll each piece into a rounded shape, about 3 inches wide. Place 3 tablespoons of filling in the center of each round. Pull up the edges around the filling. Twist to seal the top. Repeat for the remaining pieces.

8. Line a tray with parchment paper. Place the filled buns and cover with a damp towel. Let it rise for about 45 minutes.

9. Set up your steamer. Line the steamer basket with parchment paper to prevent sticking. Place the buns inside, making sure they have ample space in between. You may want to steam them in batches if your steamer is small. Steam the buns for 12 minutes. Serve warm.

Tianjin Bau

Named after the Tianjin region in China, these bau are said to have been created for the Empress Dowager Cixi herself. Certainly, the flavorful meat filling is fit for any royalty!

Makes 12 buns.

Ingredients:

Filling

- 12 oz. pork, sliced thinly
- 1 tsp. five spice powder
- ¼ cup soy sauce
- ¼ cup brown sugar
- ½ teaspoon garlic, minced
- 1 pc. star anise
- dash of salt
- 1 cup water

Directions:

1. Prepare the filling first. In a bowl, combine soy sauce, five spice powder, garlic and salt. Mix well.

2. Marinade the pork in the combined mixture for at least an hour.

3. Heat a medium-sized pot then place pork together with the marinade and water. Let it boil.

4. Add the star anise and brown sugar. Stir to distribute evenly. Simmer for 30 minutes, flipping the meat every

couple of minutes. Continue cooking over low heat until the sauce has thickened. Remove from heat and set aside.

Bau

- 1 cup warm water
- ½ cup water
- ¼ oz. active dry yeast
- 1 cup wheat flour
- 3 cups flour
- ¼ cup sugar
- 2 tbsp. shortening
- 1 ½ tsp. salt

Directions:

1. In a large bowl, stir together the warm water and yeast. Let rest for about 10 minutes to allow the yeast to proof.

2. Mix in the wheat flour into the yeast mixture until smooth. Cover with plastic wrap and set in a warm place to rise for about 1 hour.

3. Meanwhile, combine the sugar, shortening and ½ cup of water in a small saucepan. Bring to a boil over medium heat. Stir the mixture to dissolve the sugar. Remove from heat and set aside.

4. When the mixture has cooled, pour it into the batter mixture. Stir in the 3 cups of flour.

5. Lightly flour your kneading surface. Knead to form a soft, smooth dough. Place the dough into a large, greased

bowl. Cover with a damp cloth and let it rise for about an hour or until the dough has doubled in size.

6. Punch down the dough with your fist and knead gently for another couple of minutes. Divide the dough into two equal halves. Roll each half into a log.

7. Cut each log into 12 pieces. Roll each piece into a rounded shape, about 3 inches wide. Place 3 tablespoons of the filling in the center of each round. Pull up the edges around the filling. Twist to seal the top. Repeat for the remaining pieces.

8. Line a tray with parchment paper. Place the filled buns and cover with a damp towel. Let it rise for about 45 minutes.

9. Set up your steamer. Line the steamer basket with parchment paper to prevent sticking. Place the buns inside, making sure they have ample space in between. You may want to steam them in batches if your steamer is small. Steam the buns for 12 minutes. Serve warm.

Flower Rolls

Not only are these traditional dim sum bau pretty to look at, they taste great, too! Lightly flavored with scallions, they are the perfect buns to serve with tea.

Makes 12 buns.

Ingredients:

- 2 tsp. active dry yeast
- 1 ½ cups lukewarm water
- 1 tbsp. sugar
- 3 ½ cups all-purpose flour
- 2 tsp. baking powder
- 2 tsp. water
- 4 tbsp. sesame oil
- 1 tsp. salt
- ¼ cup scallions, chopped

Directions:

1. In a bowl, combine the yeast and warm water. Stir in the sugar to dissolve. Let it stand for 15 minutes.

2. Meanwhile, sift the flour in another bowl. Add the yeast mixture and begin stirring immediately. Continue stirring until the dough doesn't stick to the sides of the bowl. You may add water as needed.

3. Sprinkle flour on your working surface. Turn the dough out and knead until it is smooth and elastic. Add flour or water if needed. Cover with a cloth and let it rest for 1 1/2 hours. Punch the dough down with your fist, and let it rest again for another hour or until it has doubled in size.

4. Dissolve the baking powder in 2 teaspoons water. Knead the mixture into the dough vigorously. Continue until the dough is elastic again.

5. Roll out the dough into a large rectangle using a rolling pin. Don't make it too thin. Rub the sesame oil all over the dough. Sprinkle evenly with the salt and chopped green onions. Then, take one end of the rectangle and start rolling up the dough. Cut into 2-inch pieces.

6. With cut sides facing outward, take two pieces and press them down lengthwise in the middle. Press firmly but take care not to cut right through the dough. The layers should spread outward. Pick up the dough by its rounded ends, and pull until they meet underneath the roll. Let the rolls sit for 10 minutes. Steam the buns for 20 minutes. Serve warm.

Pork Pastry Puff

In this recipe, savory sweet roasted pork is encased in flaky, puff pastry and baked to perfection. Simply delicious!

Makes 12 pastry puffs.

Ingredients:

- 1 box (17 ounces) ready-made rolled puff pastry
- 1 egg, beaten
- Sesame seeds, for sprinkling

Filling

- 9 oz. pork tenderloin
- 4 tbsp. light soy sauce
- 2 tbsp. ginger, finely grated
- 2 tbsp. honey

- 2 tbsp. yellow soybean sauce (available in most Asian groceries)
- 1 tbsp. Shaoxing rice wine
- 3 cloves garlic, chopped
- dash of salt and pepper

Directions:

1. In a large bowl, combine the soy sauce, ginger, honey, bean sauce, rice wine and garlic. Mix well. Sprinkle with salt and pepper. Add the pork. Massage the pork with your hands to cover with the marinade. Cover with plastic wrap and refrigerate for at least 2 hours.

2. Meanwhile, pre-heat the oven to 350° F. Remove the pork from the marinade and reserve the marinade. Place the pork in a roasting pan. Roast for about 40 minutes.

3. While roasting the pork, boil the reserved marinade in a small saucepan. Remove from heat and use about 2 tablespoons to baste the pork. Let the remaining marinade cool to room temperature.

4. When the pork is cooked, remove from the oven. Let it cool down for a few minutes before slicing it into cubes. Coat the cubed pork with the reserved marinade. Set aside.

5. Pre-heat the oven to 400°F. Line a roasting tray with parchment paper.

6. Cut the puff pastry sheets into 12 equal squares. Brush the edges of each square with the beaten egg. Place a teaspoonful of the pork filling in the center of each pastry. Fold the square in half to create a triangular pastry. Pinch

edges to seal.

7. Place puffs on the roasting tray. Brush with remaining egg and sprinkle sesame seeds on top. Cook for about 20 minutes or until they turn golden brown. Serve immediately.

Other Dim Sum Delights

The following recipes are a selection of other traditional dim sum recipes. From sweet to savory, these dim sum delights will surely tickle your taste buds!

Radish Cake

A cake made out radish? Well, it's not actually the kind of cake you have in mind. Made out of grated radish or turnips, this savory, sweet-ish cake is perfect accompaniment with tea or as an appetizer.

Makes 20 slices.

Ingredients:

- 16 oz. radish, grated
- 8 oz. rice flour
- 2 ½ cups water

- 1 cup strained liquid from grated radish
- 3 tbsp. cooking oil
- 5 garlic cloves
- 1 oz. dried shrimp, soaked, squeezed, and minced
- ½ tsp. white pepper
- 1 tbsp. sugar
- ½ tsp. salt
- 2 oz. corn flour

Directions:

1. In a big bowl, combine the rice flour, water and radish liquid. Set aside.

2. Heat the cooking oil in a wok. Stir fry the garlic. Add the minced shrimp and continue stir frying for another minute.

3. Add the grated radish. Season with the pepper, sugar and salt. Stir and continue cooking over medium heat for a couple of minutes.

4. Add the rice flour and corn flour. Cook till the mixture thickens. Remove from heat and pour the mixture into square baking pans.

5. Prepare your steamer. Place the pans inside and steam over boiling water for 30 minutes. Remove from heat. Let cool to room temperature.

6. Slice into 20 even pieces. Heat a little oil in a frying pan. Pan fry each side of the cake till it turns a light, golden brown. Serve warm.

Taro Fritters

While not exactly a dumpling, taro fritters do resemble the shape and size of one. These super easy and crunchy delights are sure to be a hit!

Makes 20 pieces.

Ingredients:

- 8 oz. taro, coarsely grated
- 2 tbsp. tapioca starch
- 1 ½ tbsp. sugar
- ½ tbsp. salt
- ½ cup water
- oil for deep-frying
- sweet chili sauce

Directions:

1. In a bowl, mix together the taro, tapioca starch, sugar and salt. Mix well.

2. Shape the mixture into balls using two spoons.

3. Heat the cooking oil in a deep-fryer. Drop the taro balls into the hot oil. Do not overcrowd your fryer. Fry till golden brown. Remove from heat. Drain off excess oil using paper towels. Serve warm with sweet chili sauce.

Stuffed Tofu

Tofu is certainly one those ingredients that taste great no matter what you do with it. Fried, steamed or even eaten on its own, tofu – especially when freshly made – is always delicious! Here, tofu is stuffed with meat filling and steamed for a yummy dim sum treat.

Makes 4 servings.

Ingredients:

- 8 oz. firm tofu, cut into half diagonally
- 4 oz. ground pork
- 1/8 tsp. sugar
- ¼ tbsp. tapioca starch
- 1/8 tsp. soy sauce
- ½ stalk spring onion, chopped finely
- dash of salt and pepper

Directions:

1. Make two slits on the tofu. Remove as much tofu as you can in between slits for the stuffing. Sprinkle some salt on the tofu. Set aside.

2. In a bowl, mix together the pork, sugar, tapioca, soy sauce, spring onion, salt and pepper. Form into balls and carefully insert it into the tofu. Firm it up using your fingers.

3. Prepare your steamer. Steam the tofu for about 15 minutes. Serve warm.

Spring Onion Pancakes

Rich and crispy, these savory pancakes are a popular dim sum menu item. In China, these are also traditionally eaten as breakfast, too.

Makes 4 servings.

Ingredients:

- ¼ cup spring onion, chopped finely
- 1/8 tsp. salt
- ½ cup warm water
- 3 oz. plain flour
- 1/8 tsp. vegetable oil
- 1 tbsp. vegetable oil
- ½ tbsp. sesame oil or as needed

Directions:

1. Dissolve salt in warm water. Mix in 2 ounces of the flour to make a soft dough. Sprinkle flour on your work surface and knead the dough until slightly springy. If the dough is too sticky, knead in 1/8 teaspoon of vegetable oil. Divide the dough into 4 pieces. Cover with a cloth and set aside.

2. In a bowl, mix the remaining flour with a tablespoon of vegetable oil to make a mixture like fine crumbs.

3. Return to your dough. Roll each piece into a thin square. Brush with sesame oil and sprinkle lightly with about a teaspoon of the flour-oil mixture.

4. Sprinkle about a tablespoon of the chopped spring onions onto the dough. Spread the onion out evenly. Starting with a long end, roll the dough up into a rope shape. Pinch the seams to close the ends. Roll into a spiral, pressing lightly. Gently roll it out into a pancake shape over the floured work surface. Repeat with the remaining pancakes.

5. Heat a non-stick frying pan over medium heat. Brush your pan with vegetable oil. Fry the pancake one by one until each side turns a light, golden brown. Rove from heat. Serve warm.

San Choy Bau

This classic Chinese dim sum makes use of lettuce leaves as holder for the filling. You can opt to serve the filling already inside the lettuce leaves or for a more fun dining experience, have people put the filling while eating.

Makes 4 servings.

Ingredients:

- 8 iceberg lettuce leaves, washed and drained
- 9 oz. pork, minced
- 1½ tbsp. vegetable oil
- 2 garlic cloves, chopped
- 1½ tbsp. oyster sauce
- 2 tsp. soy sauce
- 2 tsp. sugar
- 6 oz. water chestnuts, drained and chopped
- 2 spring onions, sliced
- 2 tsp. corn starch mixed with ¼ cup water
- 1½ tbsp. hoisin sauce

Directions:

1. In a wok, heat the oil over medium-high heat. Stir fry the garlic. Add the pork and cook until it browns. Meanwhile, combine the oyster sauce, soy sauce and sugar in a small bowl.

2. Add the water chestnuts, spring onions and oyster sauce mixture to the wok. Stir vigorously. Add the cornstarch mixture. Simmer until it thickens. Remove from heat. Set aside.

3. Trim the lettuce leaves using kitchen scissors to form a cup shape. Divide the filling among the lettuce cups. Drizzle with hoisin sauce. Serve hot.

Salted Egg Yolk Prawns

Another dim sum classic is this recipe of crispy, coated prawns! Give this delicious delight a try.

Makes 4 servings.

Ingredients:

- 1 salted duck egg (available in most Asian groceries)
- 9 oz. prawns, shelled and deveined
- 1 egg
- ½ cup plain flour
- 4 tsp. cornstarch
- 1 tsp. oil (for the batter)
- ¼ cup water
- flour for dusting
- oil for deep-frying
- 1 tbsp. butter
- salt and pepper to taste
- dash of shichimi powder (Japanese chili powder)

Directions:

1. Steam the salted egg. Shell and discard the white part. Using a fork, mash the yolk. Set aside.

2. In a bowl, combine the egg, plain flour, cornstarch and oil. Pour in the water while stirring the mixture to create a batter.

3. Dust the prawns with flour. Dip each piece in the batter.

4. Heat the oil in a fryer. When the oil is hot, deep fry the prawns until they turn golden brown. Drain excess oil with paper towels.

5. In a shallow pan, heat the butter. Add the yolk and cook until bubbles form. Toss in the prawns lightly, coating them with the yolk. Season with salt and pepper. Remove from heat and transfer to serving platters. Sprinkle with shichimi. Serve hot.

Sweet Sesame Seed Balls

The sweet taste of warm, bean paste erupts in your mouth as soon as you take a bite of this crispy treat. Perfect with tea!

Makes 4 servings.

Ingredients:

- 1 cup red bean paste (available in most Asian groceries)
- ½ cup white sesame seed
- ¾ cup brown sugar
- 1 cup boiling water
- 3 cups glutinous rice flour
- oil for deep frying

Directions:

1. Dissolve the brown sugar in the boiling water. Set aside.

2. Place the rice flour in a large bowl. Make a well in the middle of the bowl and add the dissolved sugar and water mixture. Stir until you have a sticky, caramel-colored dough. Set aside.

3. Spread the sesame seeds on a parchment-lined tray. Set aside.

4. Pinch off a piece of dough roughly the size of a golf ball. Using your thumb, make a deep indentation in the dough. With your fingers, mold the dough into a cup. Fill the hole with a spoonful of sweet red bean paste. Shape the dough into a ball, closing the top over the filling to seal. Continue with the remaining dough and bean paste.

5. Roll the balls in sesame seeds. You may dip the balls in water to help the seeds stick. Repeat for the remainder of the balls.

6. Pre-heat the oil in a deep pan. Make sure that the sesame balls will be completely covered. Deep fry the balls, a few at a time. Once the sesame seeds turn light brown, use the back of a spatula to gently press the balls against the side of the pan. This will help the balls expand. Continue applying pressure until the balls itself turn golden brown. Remove from heat. Drain excess oil with paper towels. Serve warm.

Pearl Balls

With its pearl-like, sticky rice coating, these savory pork balls don't only look pretty, it tastes even better!

Makes 30 balls.

Ingredients:

- ¾ cup glutinous rice, soaked overnight
- 8 oz. ground pork
- 1 spring onion, chopped
- 2 water chestnuts, minced
- 1 egg white
- 1 tbsp. soy sauce
- 1 tbsp. dry sherry
- 1 tsp. salt
- 1 tsp. cornstarch

- pepper to taste
- Dipping sauce
- soy sauce

Directions:

1. Drain the glutinous rice and spread it out on a baking sheet. Set aside.

2. In a large bowl, combine the pork, soy sauce, sherry, green onion, water chestnuts, salt, pepper, egg white and cornstarch. Mix well.

3. Form the pork mixture into 1 inch balls. Roll each ball lightly over the glutinous rice and place on a heatproof plate. Continue until you have no more pork mixture left.

4. Prepare the steamer. Steam the pearl balls for 20 - 35 minutes or until they are cooked through. Serve warm with soy sauce.

Shrimp Toast

This is another popular dim sum on most Chinese restaurants. The crispy toast topped with flavorful shrimp is always a sure-fire hit!

Makes 4 servings.

Ingredients:

- 4 slices white bread, crusts removed
- 6 oz. shrimp, peeled and deveined
- 2 tsp. lard
- 2 water chestnuts, chopped
- ½ tomato, chopped
- 2 green onions, chopped
- 1 tsp. ginger, grated
- 1 tsp. white rice vinegar
- 1 egg, lightly beaten
- salt and pepper, to taste
- 2 tsp. cornstarch

- oil for deep frying

Directions:

1. Pre-heat the oven to 225°Fahrenheit.

2. Cut each slice of bread diagonally to form 4 triangles. Place the bread on a non-stick baking sheet. Bake for 30 minutes or until the bread is completely dry.

3. Meanwhile, prepare the filling. Place in the food processor the shrimp and the lard. Process until the shrimp is chopped into little chunks.. Add the water chestnut, tomato, green onion and ginger. Process again. The, add the rice wine or vinegar, beaten egg, salt, pepper and cornstarch. Process until the mixture becomes paste-like.

4. Take your toast slices and spread the shrimp mixture on top. Repeat for the remaining slices.

5. In a wok, heat enough oil for deep frying. Deep fry toast slices, shrimp side down. Cook each side for about 2 minutes before turning to the other side. Serve warm.

Clam Sycee

A Shanghai original, this recipe is popularly served as a New Years dim sum fare. But of course, youre free to enjoy it any time of the year!

Makes 4 servings.

Ingredients:

- 2 dozen clams, cleaned
- 2 tsp. olive oil
- ½ cup dry white wine
- 2 tbsp. Shaoxing rice
- 1 ginger, sliced
- 1 green onion, sliced
- 1 tbsp. cornstarch dissolved in 2 tbsp. water
- ¾ cup chicken stock
- 1 tbsp. oyster sauce
- 2 tbsp. soy sauce
- 1 tsp. sugar
- 4 oz. ground pork
- 1 tbsp. cornstarch
- salt to taste
- oil for deep frying

Directions:

1. Heat the olive oil in a wok over medium high heat. Add a tablespoon of the Shaoxing wine, ginger, green onion, and clams. Cover and cook until the clams open. Remove the clams from heat. Let cool. Do not clean out the pan.

2. Meanwhile, combine the chicken broth, oyster sauce, a

tablespoon of the soy sauce and sugar in a bowl. Add the cornstarch and water mixture. Heat the mixture until it thickens. Set aside.

3. Shuck the clams, setting aside the shells for later use. Mince the clam meat. Mix the clam with the ground pork. Stir in the remaining Shaoxing wine and soy sauce. Add cornstarch and salt.

4. Take your clam half shells and stuff it with the clam and pork mixture. Repeat for the remaining clams.

5. Heat oil in your fryer. Taking a few at a time, deep fry the clams, meat side down, until they turn golden brown. Drain off excess oil with paper towels.

6. To serve, arrange in a platter and pour the prepared sauce over. Serve hot.

Printed in Great Britain
by Amazon.co.uk, Ltd.,
Marston Gate.